THE BOSTON RED SOX

Sloan MacRae

PowerKiDS press™

New York

Published in 2010 by The Rosen Publishing Group, Inc.
29 East 21st Street, New York, NY 10010

First Edition

Editor: Amelie von Zumbusch
Book Design: Greg Tucker
Photo Researcher: Jessica Gerweck

Photo Credits: Cover (Fenway Park) Shutterstock.com; cover (David Ortiz) Otto Greule Jr./Getty Images; cover (Cy Young), p. 9 Mark Rucker/Transcendental Graphics/Getty Images; cover (Ted Williams), pp. 13, 22 (top) Photo File/MLB Photos via Getty Images; cover (Carl Yaztrzemski), p. 15 Herb Scharfman/Sports Imagery/Getty Images; pp. 5, 22 (bottom) Stephen Dunn/Getty Images; p. 7 Christian Petersen/Getty Images; p. 11 © Bettman/Corbis; p. 17 Focus on Sport/Getty Images; p.19 Jed Jacobson/Getty Images; p. 21 Jim Rogash/Getty Images.

Library of Congress Cataloging-in-Publication Data

MacRae, Sloan.
  The Boston Red Sox / Sloan MacRae. — 1st ed.
     p. cm. — (America's greatest teams)
  Includes index.
  ISBN 978-1-4042-8130-1 (library binding) — ISBN 978-1-4358-3392-0 (pbk.) —
ISBN 978-1-4358-3393-7 (6-pack)
  1. Boston Red Sox (Baseball team—History—Juvenile literature. I. Title.
  GV875.B62M23 2010
  796.357'640974461—dc22
                                             2009005755

Manufactured in the United States of America

CONTENTS

CURSES CAN BE BROKEN

Are you **superstitious**? Do you believe in good and bad luck? The Boston Red Sox and their fans believe in luck of both kinds. They believe that their team was **cursed** for 86 years. That is how long the Red Sox went between winning World Series **championships**. For a while, it looked like the Red Sox might never win a championship again. Their fans kept hoping, though!

The Red Sox are one of the oldest teams in baseball. The team is rich in **traditions**. Their history and traditions make the Red Sox one of the most-loved sports teams in the world.

The Red Sox were filled with joy when their bad luck ended on October 27, 2004. This was when they won the World Series for the first time in 86 years.

5

THE GREEN MONSTER

The Red Sox play in a stadium called Fenway Park. Fenway is the oldest ballpark in Major League Baseball. The stadium has a giant green wall in left field called the Green Monster. It is the tallest wall in any major-league baseball stadium. It is extra hard to hit home runs in Fenway thanks to the Green Monster.

The Red Sox are lucky to have some of the most **loyal** fans in baseball. Boston fans are definitely not fair-weather fans. Red Sox fans root for their team no matter what. The Red Sox have had some heartbreaking seasons. However, their fans never lost **faith** in their team.

The Green Monster, seen here, was built in the 1930s. The wall did not earn its nickname until after it was painted green in 1947, though.

THE FIRST WORLD SERIES

Do you know why we call the team the Red Sox? It is because they wear red socks! The team formed in 1901 and was first called the Boston Americans. By 1907, the Americans were better known by their nickname. Everyone called them the Red Sox.

The Americans were one of the best teams around in the early 1900s. They had a star pitcher named Cy Young. Young was so good that today there is an award named after him. Each year, baseball's best pitchers win the Cy Young Award. Young and the Americans beat the Pittsburgh Pirates in the 1903 World Series. This was the very first World Series.

Cy Young pitched in four games in the first World Series. His great pitching helped the Red Sox beat the Pittsburgh Pirates, 5 games to 3.

THE CURSE OF THE BAMBINO

The Red Sox won the World Series again in 1912, 1915, 1916, and 1918. However, their luck soon changed. In 1920, the Sox dealt Babe Ruth to the New York Yankees. Ruth became baseball's biggest star. New York went on to win more World Series than any other team in baseball, but Boston would not win another World Series for many years. The Yankees often stopped the Red Sox from reaching the World Series. This caused a big **rivalry** between the two teams.

Babe Ruth's nickname was the Bambino. Baseball fans called the Sox's bad luck the Curse of the Bambino since the team kept losing after sending Ruth to the Yankees.

Babe Ruth, seen here, played for the Red Sox from 1914 to 1919. Ruth hit a total of 49 home runs during his time with the Red Sox.

TED WILLIAMS

The Red Sox may have had trouble winning a World Series, but they had great players. Ted Williams was one of the greatest of all time. Many experts believe that Williams was the best hitter ever to swing a bat. In 1941, Williams finished the season with a .406 **batting average**. No other player has ever done this since.

Williams might have been able to set other baseball records, but he missed several seasons while he was serving in the Marines. Williams was a pilot in World War II and the Korean War. He returned to baseball and kept playing until 1960. Williams even hit a home run in his last game!

In both 1942 and 1947, Williams led the league in batting average, runs batted in, and home runs. This is known as the batting Triple Crown.

13

THE IMPOSSIBLE DREAM

The Red Sox struggled in the early 1960s. They had one of their worst seasons ever in 1966. In 1967, though, they bounced back. Superstar Carl Yastrzemski led the team to its second American League championship in over 30 years. It looked like the Sox might win another World Series at last!

Fans called the 1967 season the Impossible Dream, after a song in a Broadway musical. The Sox had had bad luck for so long that winning the World Series seemed like an impossible dream. Yastrzemski helped Boston reach the World Series, but the Sox lost to the St. Louis Cardinals. It looked like the curse might be real.

Carl Yastrzemski joined the Red Sox in 1961 and became one of the team's biggest stars. He was both a powerful hitter and a skilled left fielder.

15

THE CURSE OF BILL BUCKNER

The Red Sox had some luck in the 1970s but played poorly in the early 1980s. By 1986, though, they were once again a great team. They had great pitchers, such as Roger Clemens, and great hitters, such as Wade Boggs. Could 1986 be the year Boston won a championship again?

The Sox advanced through the **postseason** and faced the New York Mets in the World Series. Boston won three games and found themselves one **strike** away from winning it all in Game Six of the series. Then, first baseman Bill Buckner missed an easy ground ball. The Mets came back, won the series, and broke the hearts of many Red Sox fans.

The sixth game of the World Series had already gone into a tenth, or extra, inning when the ball slipped through Buckner's legs.

THE IDIOTS

Up until the mid-2000s, Red Sox fans began to think that the curse on their team might never be broken. The Yankees once again ended Boston's World Series hopes in the 2003 postseason. The Sox came back in 2004 with a new **manager**, Terry Francona. They also had star pitchers Pedro Martinez and Curt Schilling and great hitters, such as Manny Ramirez, David Ortiz, and Johnny Damon.

The 2004 Red Sox called themselves the Idiots because they did not believe in curses. The Idiots became the first team in baseball history to overcome a three-game **deficit** in the postseason. They also broke the curse and **swept** the Cardinals in the World Series.

Manny Ramirez, seen here, played so well in the 2004 World Series that he was named the World Series Most Valuable Player, or MVP.

THE TEAM OF THE NEW CENTURY

Fans wondered if it would take the Red Sox another 86 years to win their next championship. As it turned out, it would take them only 3 years! Boston beat the Colorado Rockies in the 2007 World Series. Today, the Sox are one of the most successful teams in baseball.

Red Sox fans are patient. They never give up hope. They waited 86 years for their team to break the Curse of the Bambino. Some of the greatest stars in baseball history have played in Boston. Many baseball stars of tomorrow will call Fenway Park their home, too. Red Sox fans will always believe in their team.

Boston held a parade for the Red Sox after they won the 2007 World Series. Here, Red Sox player Jason Varitek holds up the World Series trophy at the parade.

21

BOSTON RED SOX TIMELINE

1903

The Boston Americans beat the Pittsburgh Pirates in the first World Series.

1912

The Sox move into Fenway Park.

1920

Babe Ruth is dealt to the Yankees. The Curse of the Bambino is said to have begun.

1941

Ted Williams hits .406.

1953

The Red Sox score 17 runs in a single inning against the Detroit Tigers.

1960

Ted Williams bats in his last game and hits a home run.

1991

Pitcher Roger Clemens wins his third Cy Young Award with the Red Sox.

2001

Superstar slugger, or hitter, Manny Ramirez joins the team.

2004

The Red Sox win the World Series for the first time in 86 years.

2007

The Red Sox win another World Series.

GLOSSARY

BATTING AVERAGE (BA-ting A-veh-rij) The number of hits a baseball player gets divided by the number of times the player is at bat.

CHAMPIONSHIPS (CHAM-pee-un-ships) Games held to decide the best, or the winner.

CURSED (KURSD) Made to suffer.

DEFICIT (DEH-fuh-sut) The amount of something that needs to be made up.

FAITH (FAYTH) A belief without proof.

LOYAL (LOY-ul) True to a person or an idea.

MANAGER (MA-nih-jer) The person in charge of the players on a team.

POSTSEASON (pohst-SEE-zun) Games played after the regular season.

RIVALRY (RY-vul-ree) A struggle between two people or things to see which one is the best.

STRIKE (STRYK) A pitch a batter misses, hits in the wrong direction, or should have tried to hit.

SUPERSTITIOUS (soo-per-STIH-shus) Believing in something that cannot be explained.

SWEPT (SWEPT) Won all stages of a game or series.

TRADITIONS (truh-DIH-shunz) Ways of doing things that have been passed down over time.

INDEX

WEB SITES

Due to the changing nature of Internet links, PowerKids Press has developed an online list of Web sites related to the subject of this book. This site is updated regularly. Please use this link to access the list:
www.powerkidslinks.com/teams/redsox/